I dedicate this book, with love, respect, and admiration, to all the children of the world who, with courage and character, know how to defend integrity and their own values and those of others.

To them, who with simplicity and love show the value of empathy and respect to all their classmates and peers wherever they may be.

To all parents, mothers, fathers, teachers, and caregivers of children. To every adult who educates with patience, love, discipline, justi-ce, and respect.

To my entire family, especially to my nieces and nephews and my children, to each and every one of you, thank you.

Children are innocent, children are impor-tant, children should not be mistreated. Chil-dren are untouchable. Children all over the world have equal rights. Children deserve only love, fair, and kind treatment.

Títle:
My friend Santiago.

Writer: Monica Santibañez
Ilustrator: Verove Pinto

ISBN: 9798325808197
Independently published
Carnaval Editorial
+1 (385) 306-9814
www.carnavaleditorial.com
contacto@carnavaleditorial.com

First Edition
Printed in USA

Written by Monica Santibañez

Illustrated by Verove Pinto

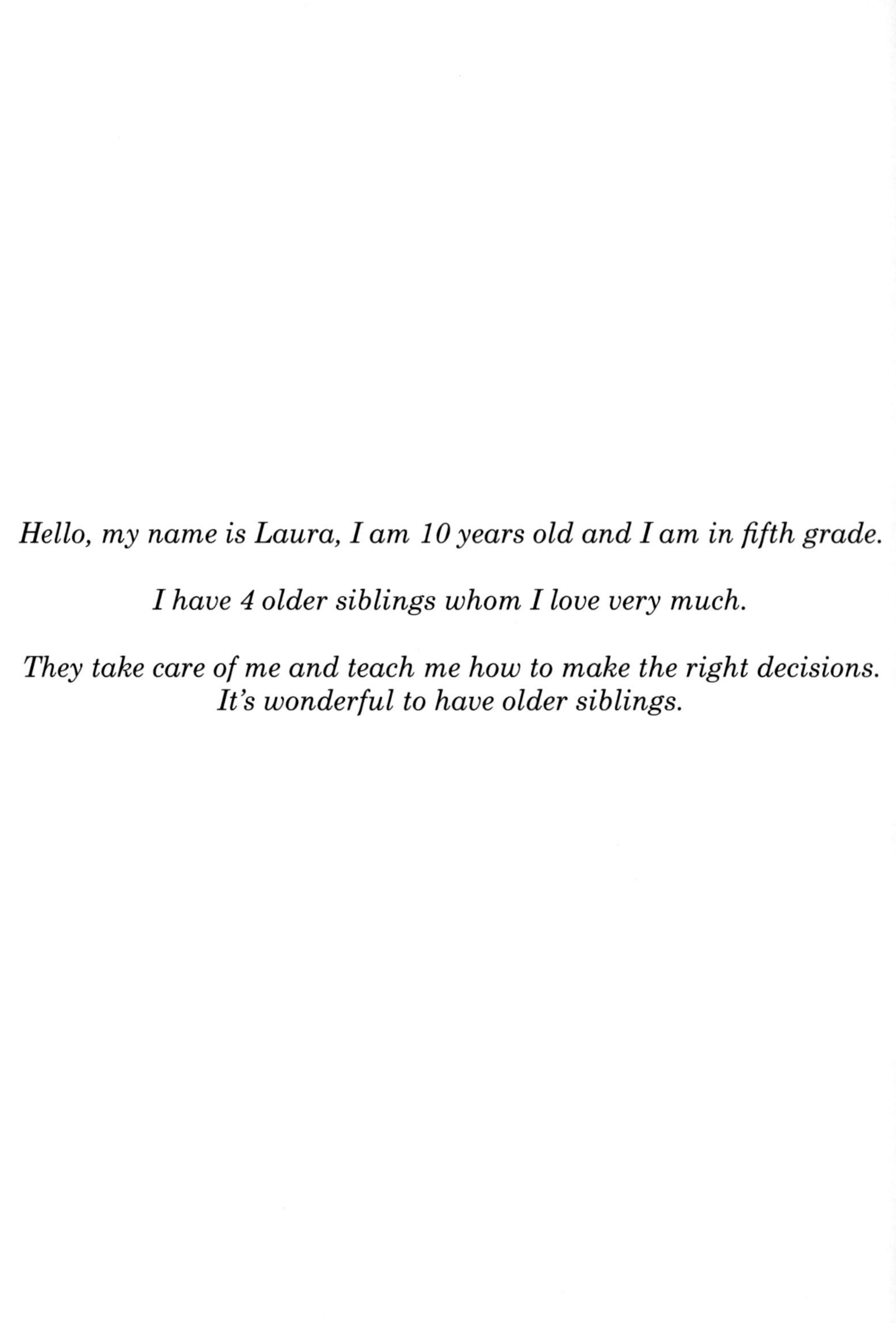

Hello, my name is Laura, I am 10 years old and I am in fifth grade.

I have 4 older siblings whom I love very much.

They take care of me and teach me how to make the right decisions. It's wonderful to have older siblings.

My mother's name is Aurora and my father's name is Daniel.
My mother is a music teacher and my father is a pediatrician.

My father says that taking care of children is one of the noblest and most beautiful acts of humanity. He also says that all adults are responsible for taking care of them, and teach them about love and respect.

My mother gives piano and violin lessons to a group of young people in the city.
It's very beautiful to see how much they love music.
Well, when I see the smiles of joy on their faces, I can tell that they enjoy it.

Every year at Christmas my mother organizes a group of young people to go to the homes of the older neighbors and sing some Christmas songs. It fills me with joy.

See how with a simple gesture of love you can
fill someone's heart.
They kindly thank you while still gifting smiles.

My mother says that this is the magic of music and the power of empathy.

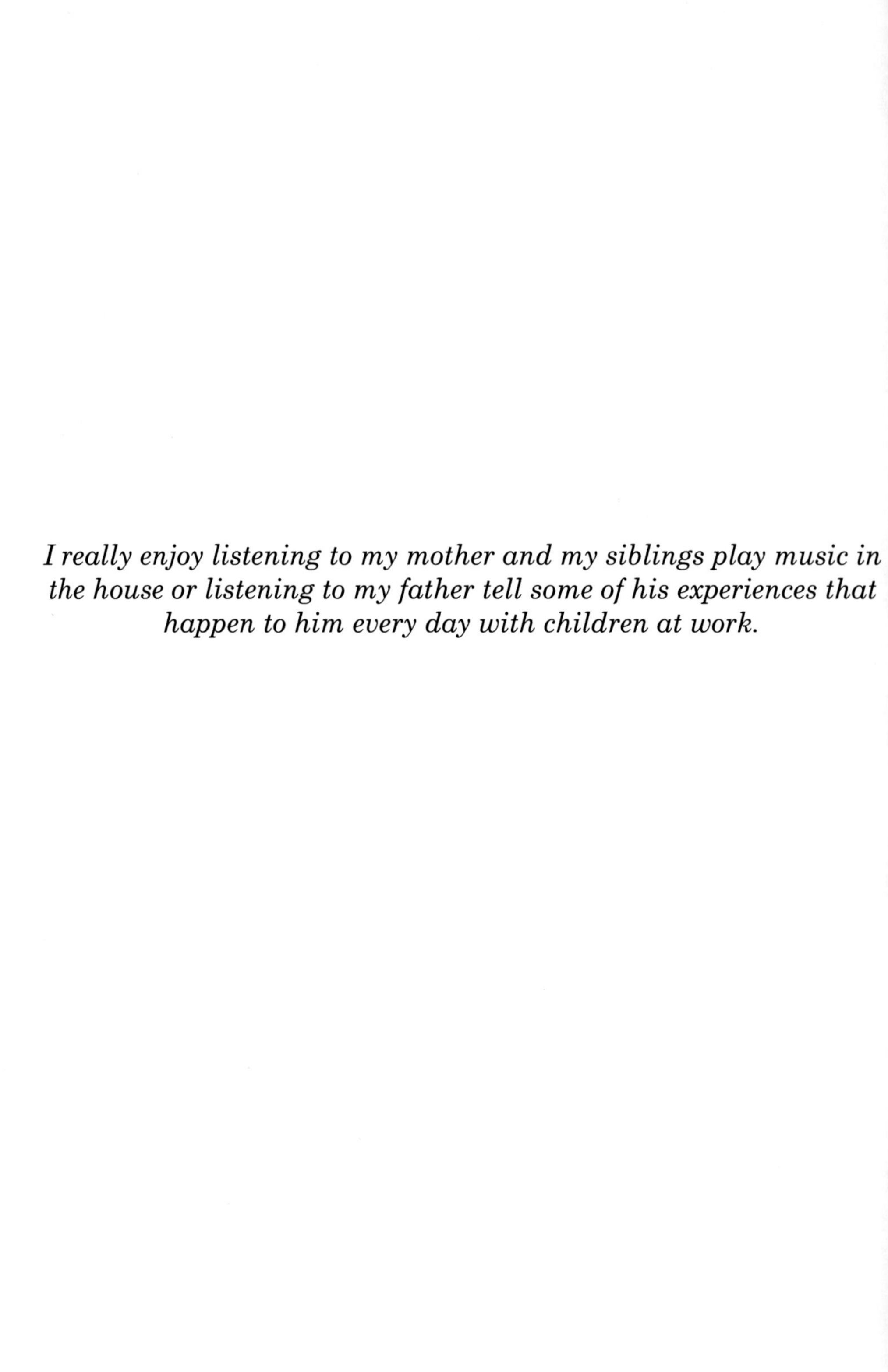

I really enjoy listening to my mother and my siblings play music in the house or listening to my father tell some of his experiences that happen to him every day with children at work.

My father says that music and books create magic. And yes, I believe him!

That's why I love going to school because my teacher reads wonderful stories that happened somewhere far away and, in my imagination, I travel to that faraway place and live that story from my own reality.

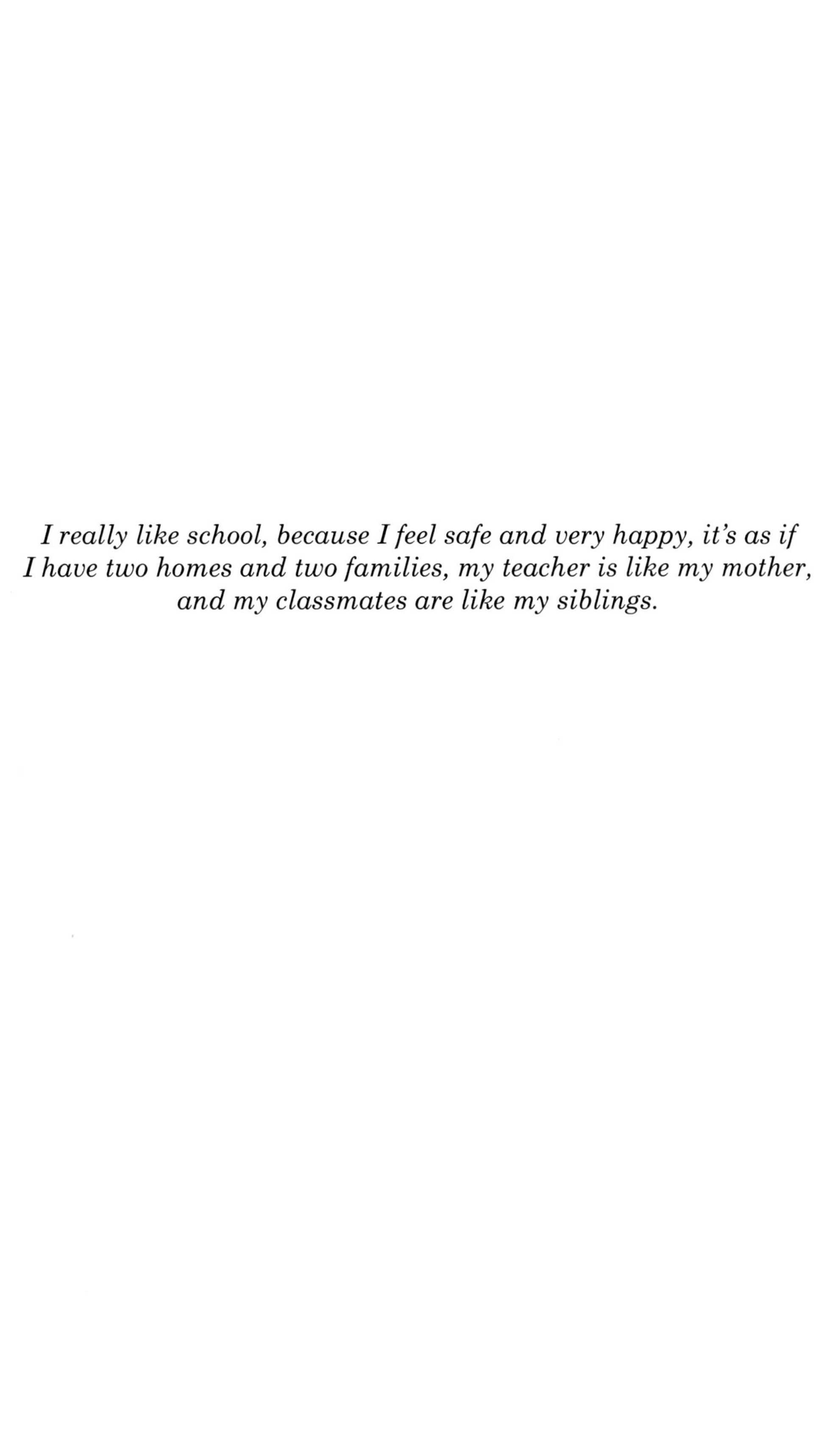

I really like school, because I feel safe and very happy, it's as if I have two homes and two families, my teacher is like my mother, and my classmates are like my siblings.

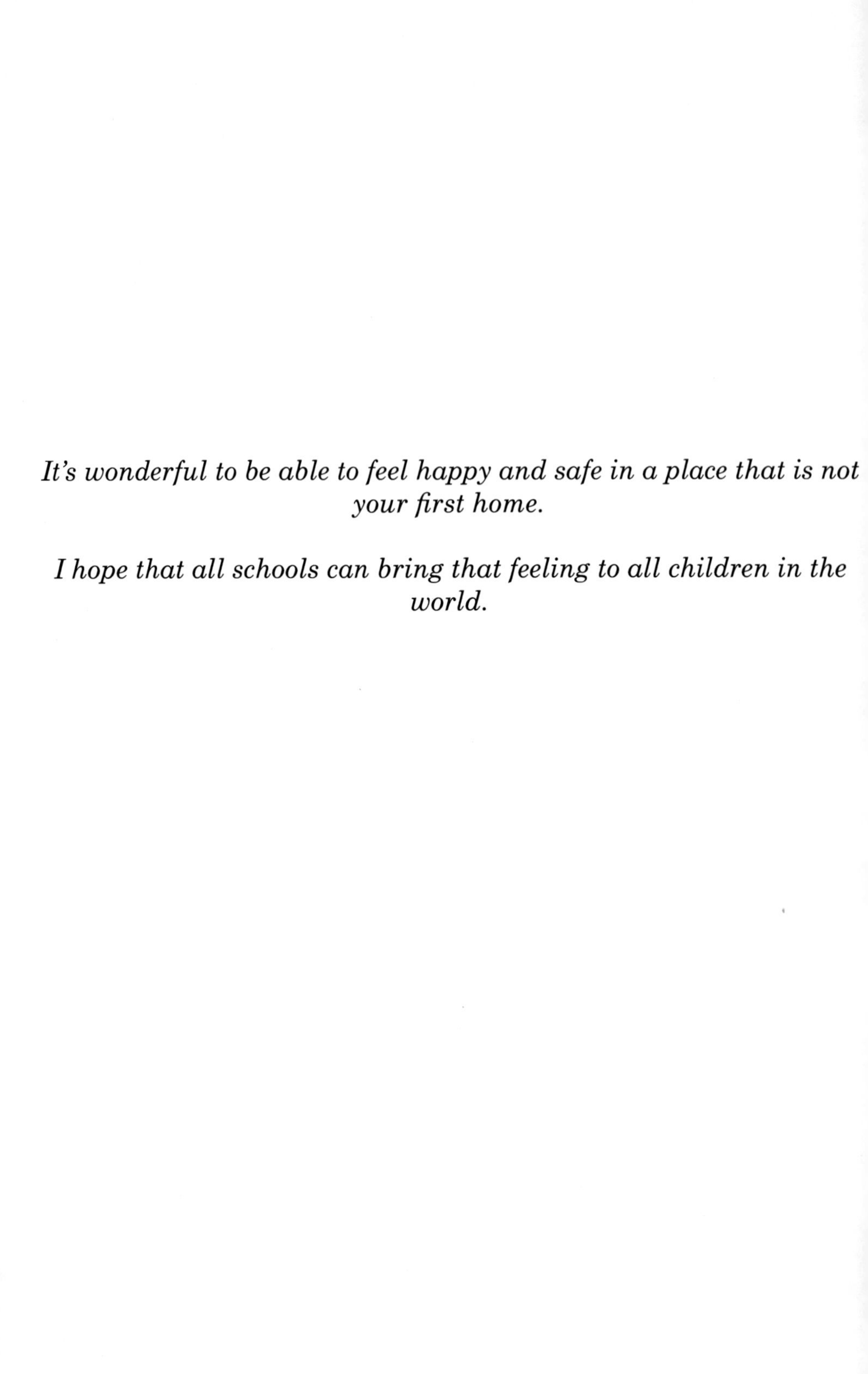

It's wonderful to be able to feel happy and safe in a place that is not your first home.

I hope that all schools can bring that feeling to all children in the world.

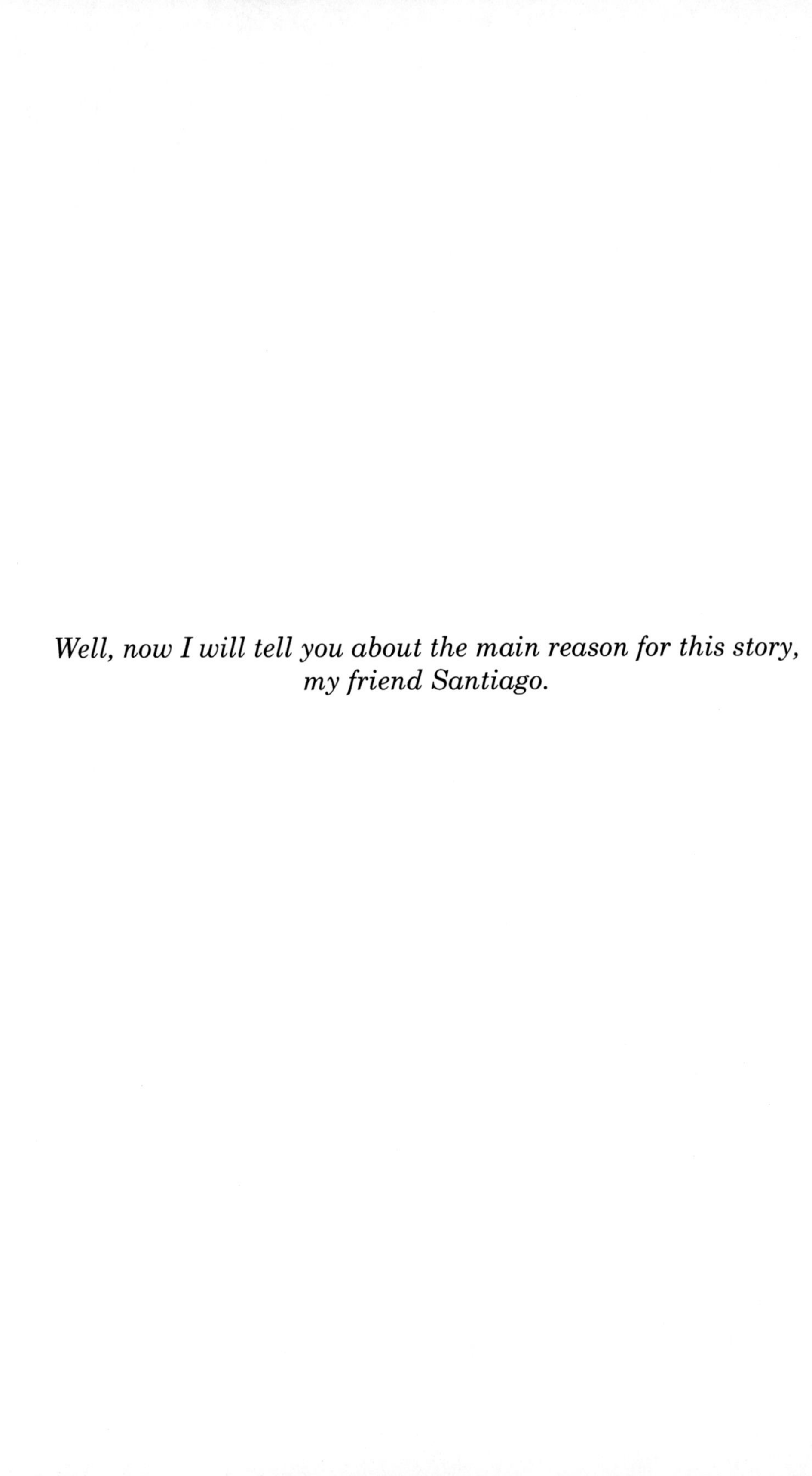

Well, now I will tell you about the main reason for this story, my friend Santiago.

Santiago arrived at school two months ago.
He is a very quiet and lonely boy.
But he has the most beautiful eyes I've ever seen
and his hair looks like the light of the sun.

Santiago is very shy and isn't often seen smiling, but when he smiles it's like watching the spring flowers bloom.

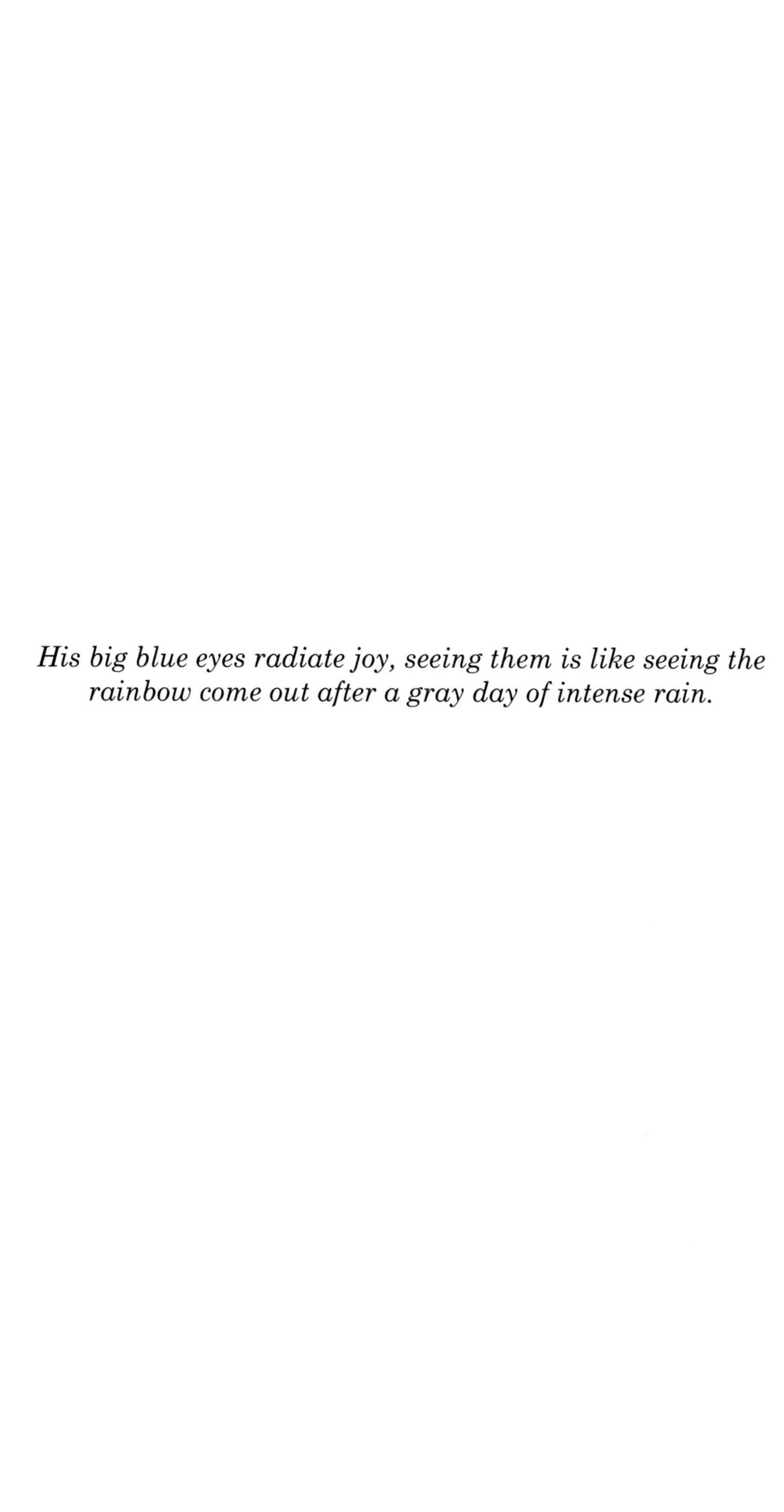

His big blue eyes radiate joy, seeing them is like seeing the rainbow come out after a gray day of intense rain.

Days ago, I watched how a sixth grade boy pushed my friend Santiago, while he said some offensive words, and pulled his blue shirt, which his grandmother had given him on his birthday.

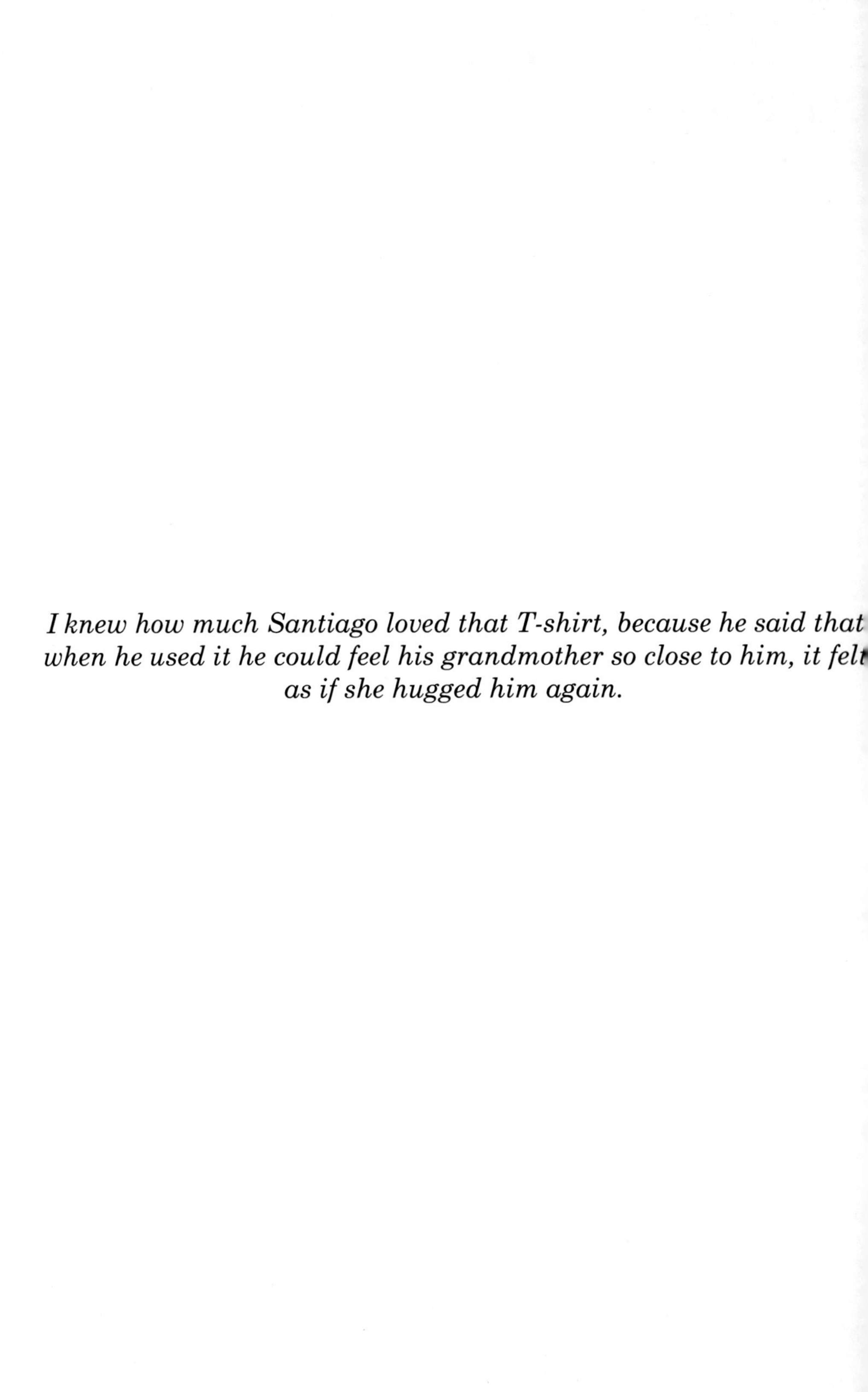

I knew how much Santiago loved that T-shirt, because he said that when he used it he could feel his grandmother so close to him, it felt as if she hugged him again.

Santiago lost his grandmother 5 months ago.
Because of his father's work, they were out of the country and he could not say goodbye to her.

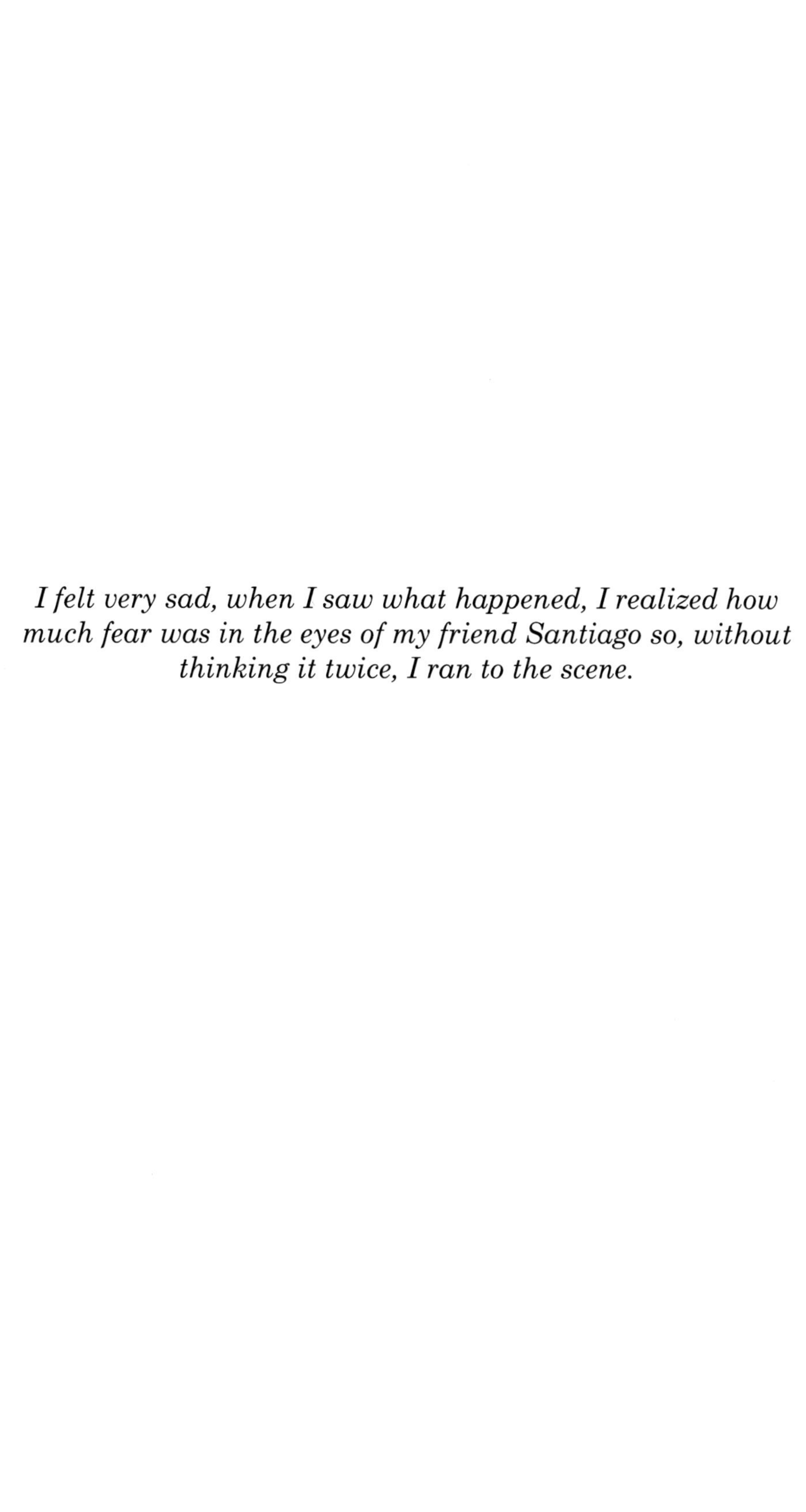

I felt very sad, when I saw what happened, I realized how much fear was in the eyes of my friend Santiago so, without thinking it twice, I ran to the scene.

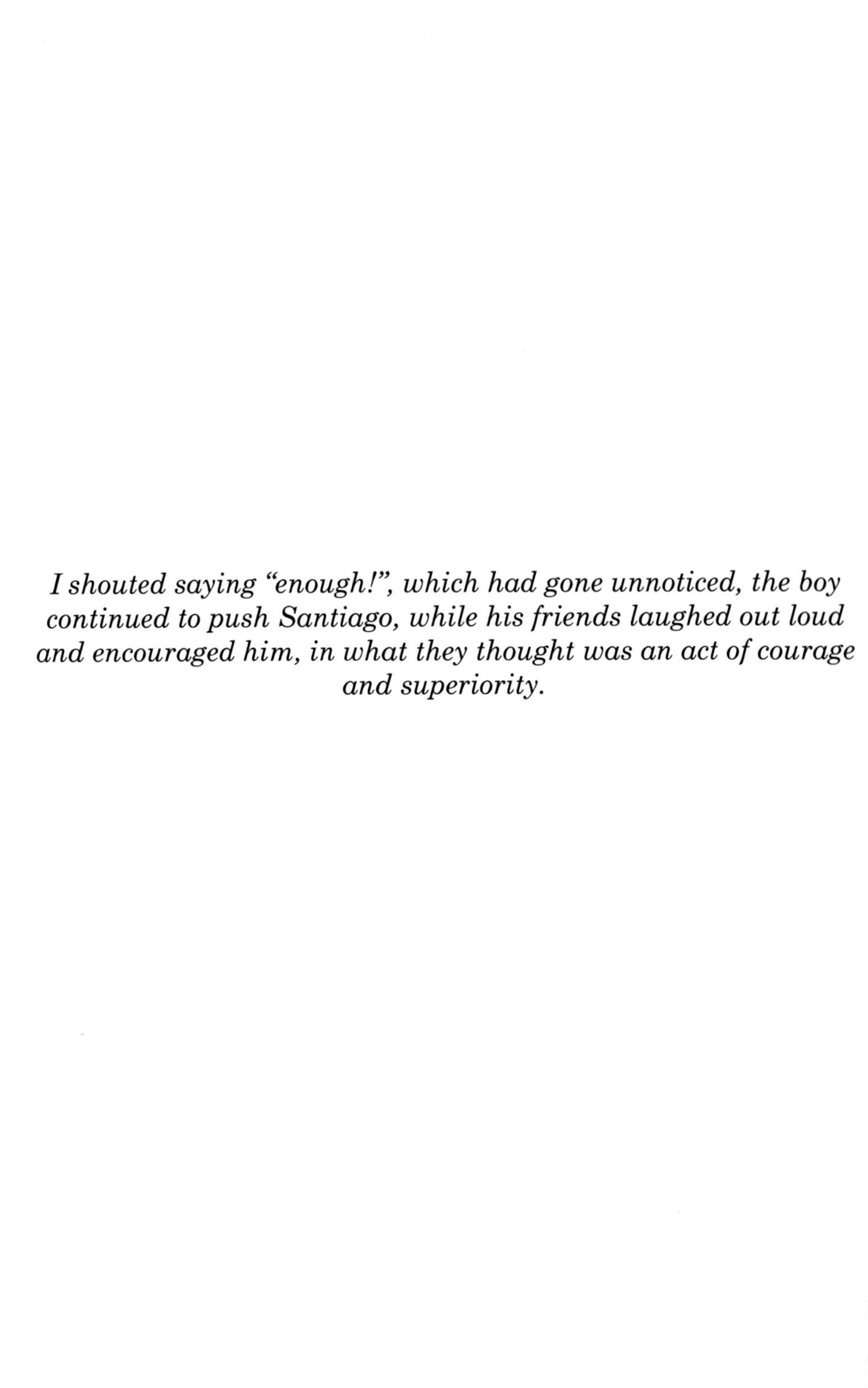

I shouted saying "enough!", which had gone unnoticed, the boy continued to push Santiago, while his friends laughed out loud and encouraged him, in what they thought was an act of courage and superiority.

It was one of the saddest scenes I had ever witnessed, because I watched my helpless and good friend be bullied by children just like him and me.

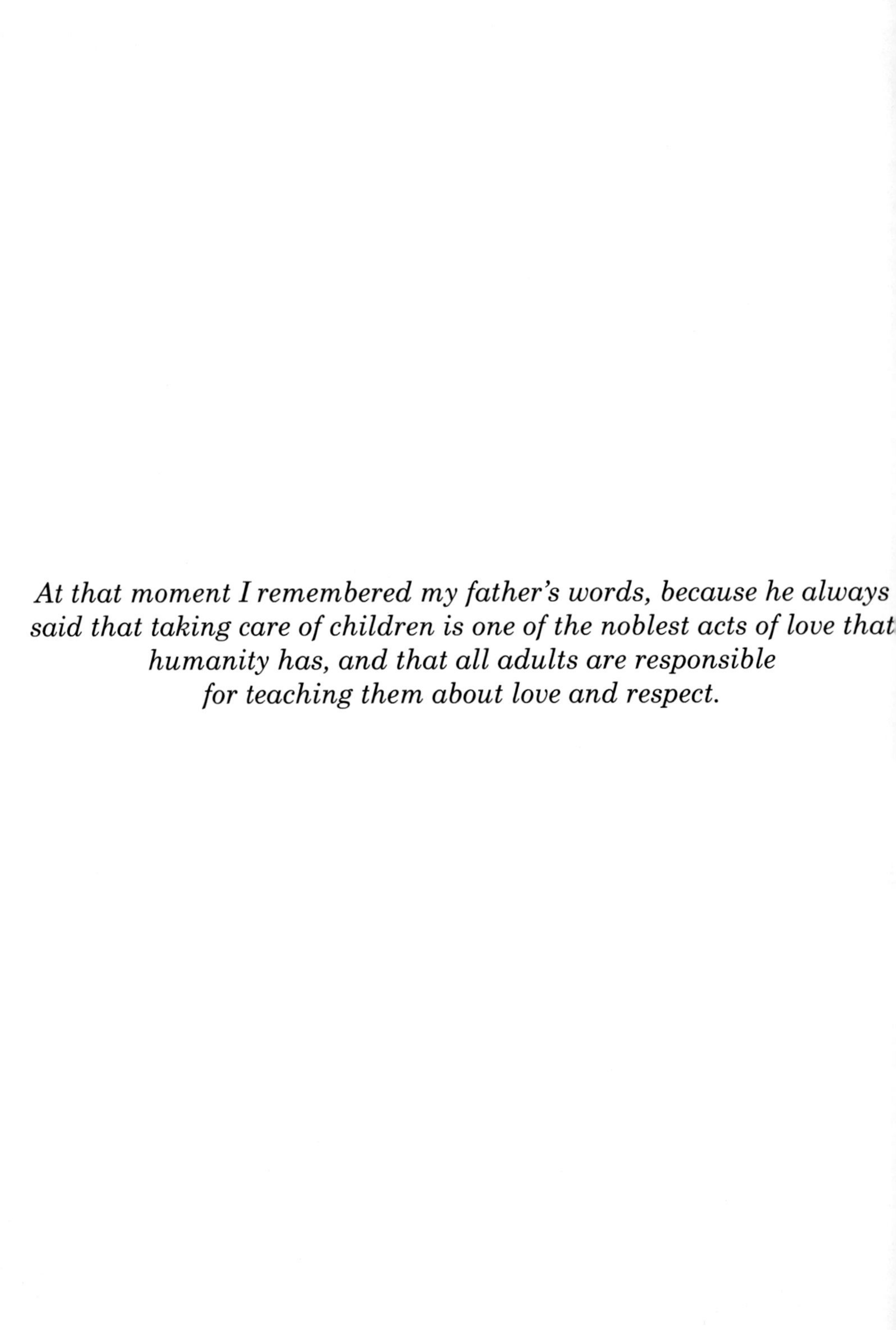

At that moment I remembered my father's words, because he always said that taking care of children is one of the noblest acts of love that humanity has, and that all adults are responsible for teaching them about love and respect.

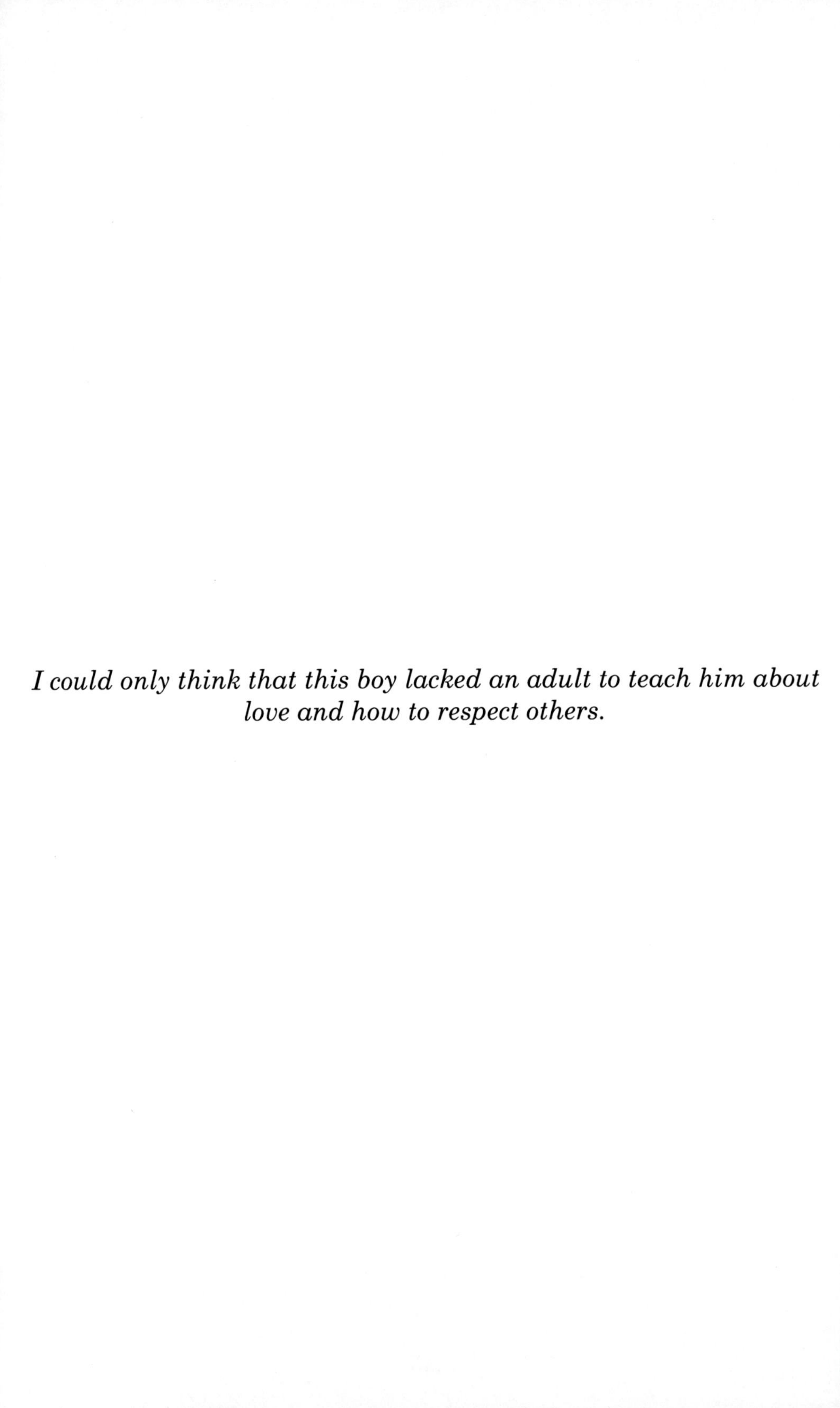

I could only think that this boy lacked an adult to teach him about love and how to respect others.

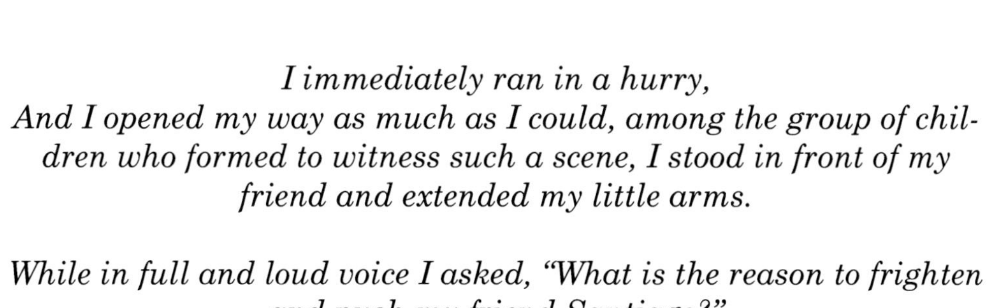

I immediately ran in a hurry,
And I opened my way as much as I could, among the group of children who formed to witness such a scene, I stood in front of my friend and extended my little arms.

While in full and loud voice I asked, "What is the reason to frighten and push my friend Santiago?"

After a few seconds of silence.
The boy laughed loudly and answered me in a mocking way, saying:

"Girl, are you blind? You don't see that he's different? Look at that huge mole on his face, it looks like a giant blackberry."

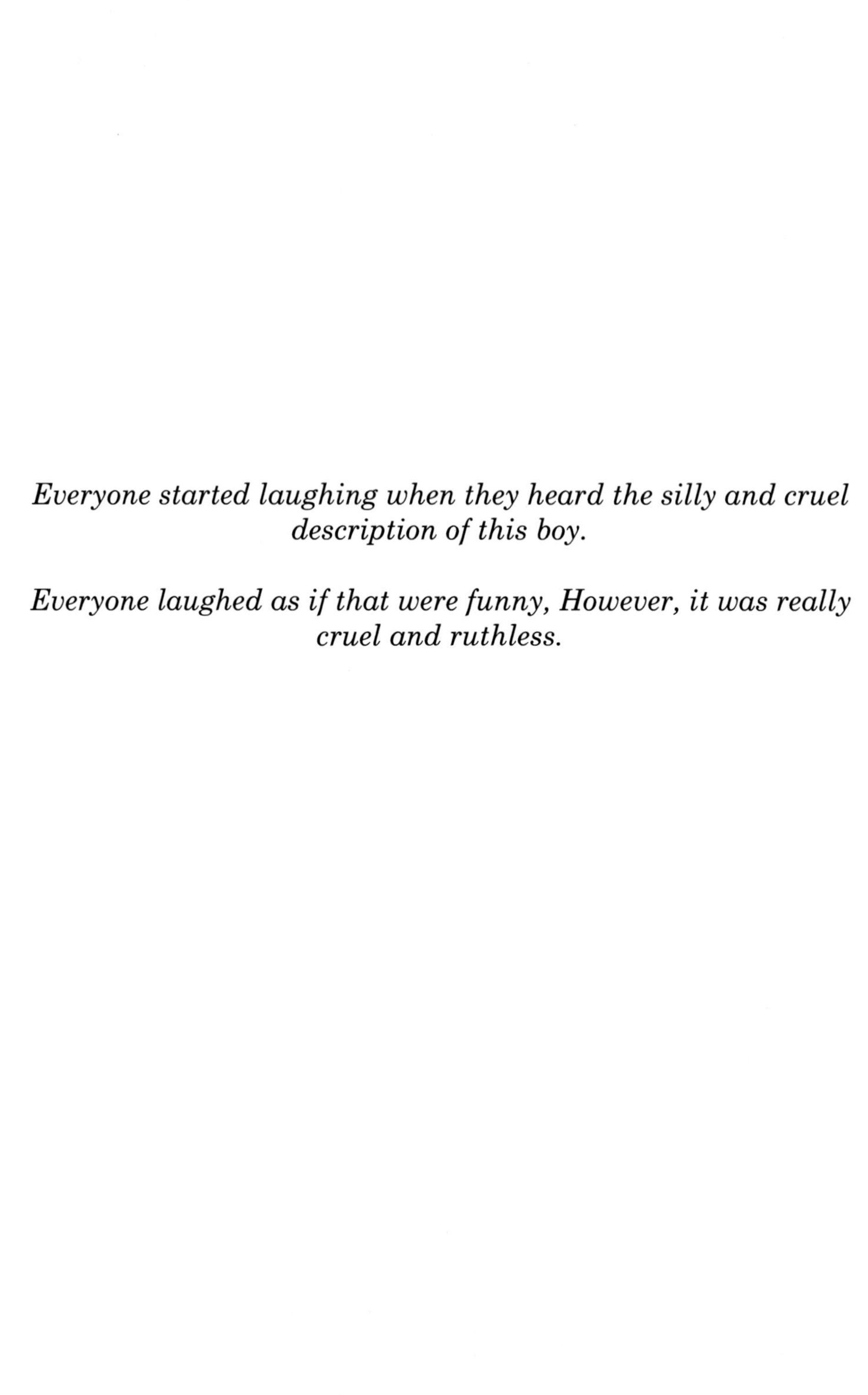

Everyone started laughing when they heard the silly and cruel description of this boy.

Everyone laughed as if that were funny, However, it was really cruel and ruthless.

HA
HA
HA

Since the beginning I did not say anything about my friend's mole, for me it is the least important thing, in fact it's beautiful to me.

What makes us different is what truly gives us value and strengthens us as human beings.

Can you imagine if we were all the same?
I don't think we would be so interesting!
Don't you think?

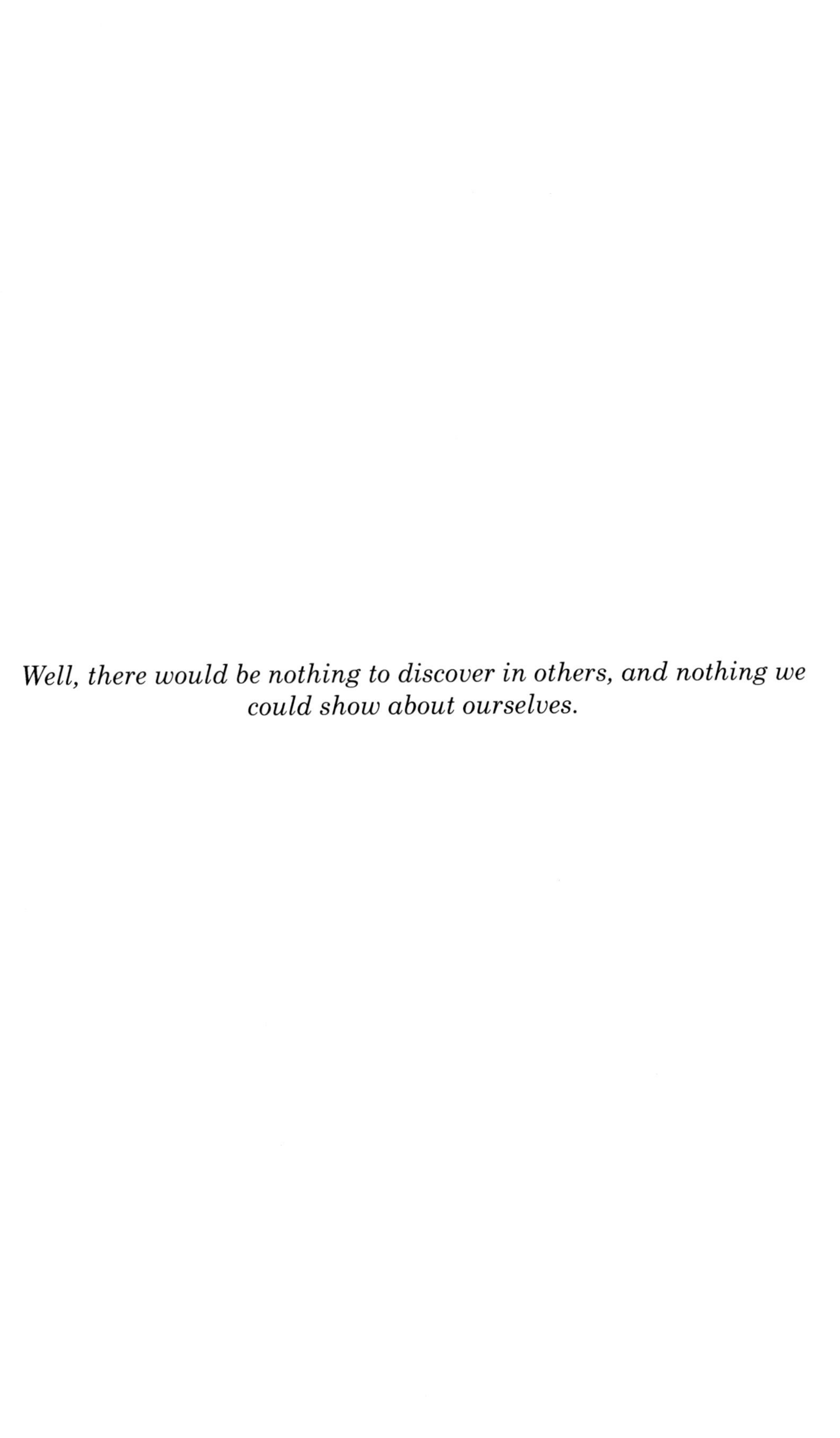

Well, there would be nothing to discover in others, and nothing we could show about ourselves.

Well, going back to the story, I asked the boy:

"What bothers you about his mole?"

He answered me saying:

"Girl, you really must be blind, what don't you see?

That huge mole is ugly and black."

I asked him, "Do you know what color the night is?"

"Do you know that there are black fruits?"

"Do you know that there are black flowers?"

"Do you know what makes the color black magical and beautiful?"

He didn't answer, because he had no answer.
He remained completely silent like the other children.

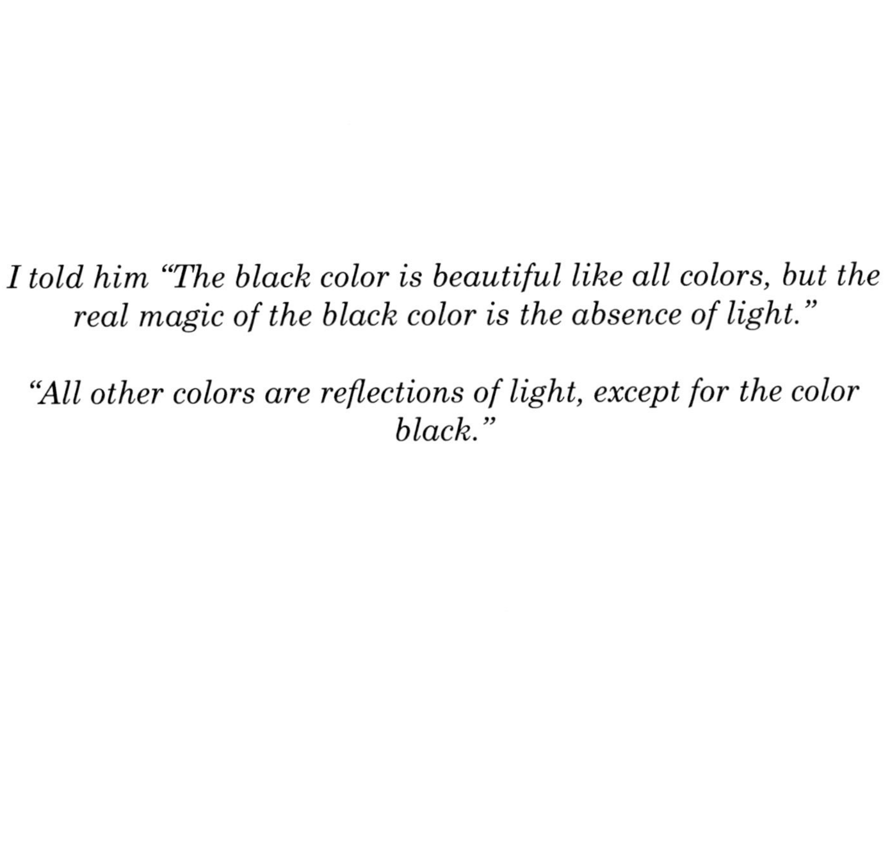

I told him "The black color is beautiful like all colors, but the real magic of the black color is the absence of light."

"All other colors are reflections of light, except for the color black."

"The night is black and that makes it beautiful, because it is full of mystery and shows us the reality of a natural event, it teaches us that there is opposition and it is fine!"

"Well, we all think differently and we will not always agree with the ideas of others, but that is no reason to fill ourselves with hatred or anger against someone or something."

love

"Night and day are very opposite and both are beautiful and show us the beauty that each one possesses, both marvel at their charms and each one has its magic and shows it in its own time without envy."

“Black fruits also have their charm, as they are delicious and sweet.”

¿"Who doesn't enjoy a delicious salad with black olives? Or who can resist a delicious blackberry jam?"

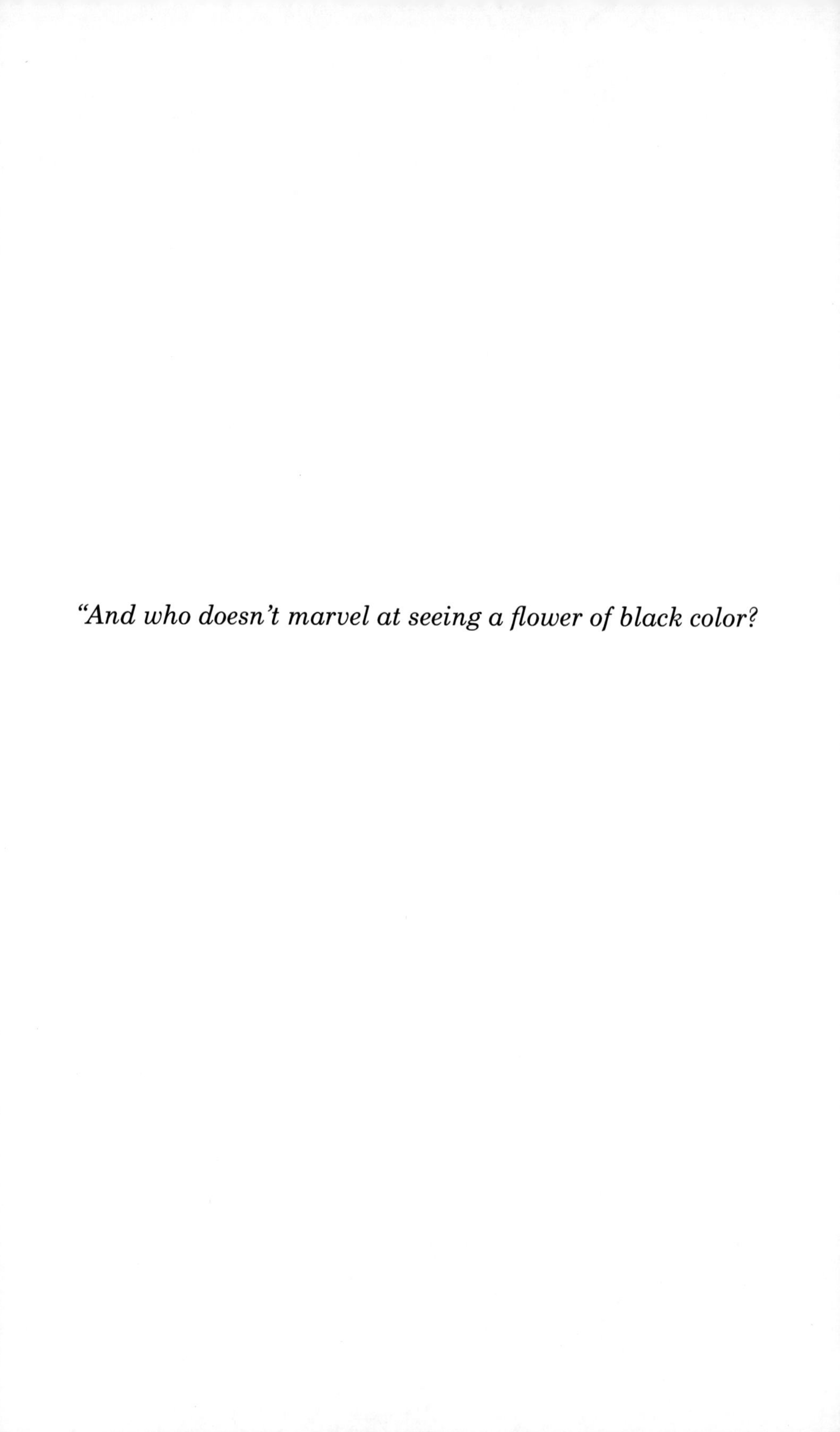

“And who doesn’t marvel at seeing a flower of black color?

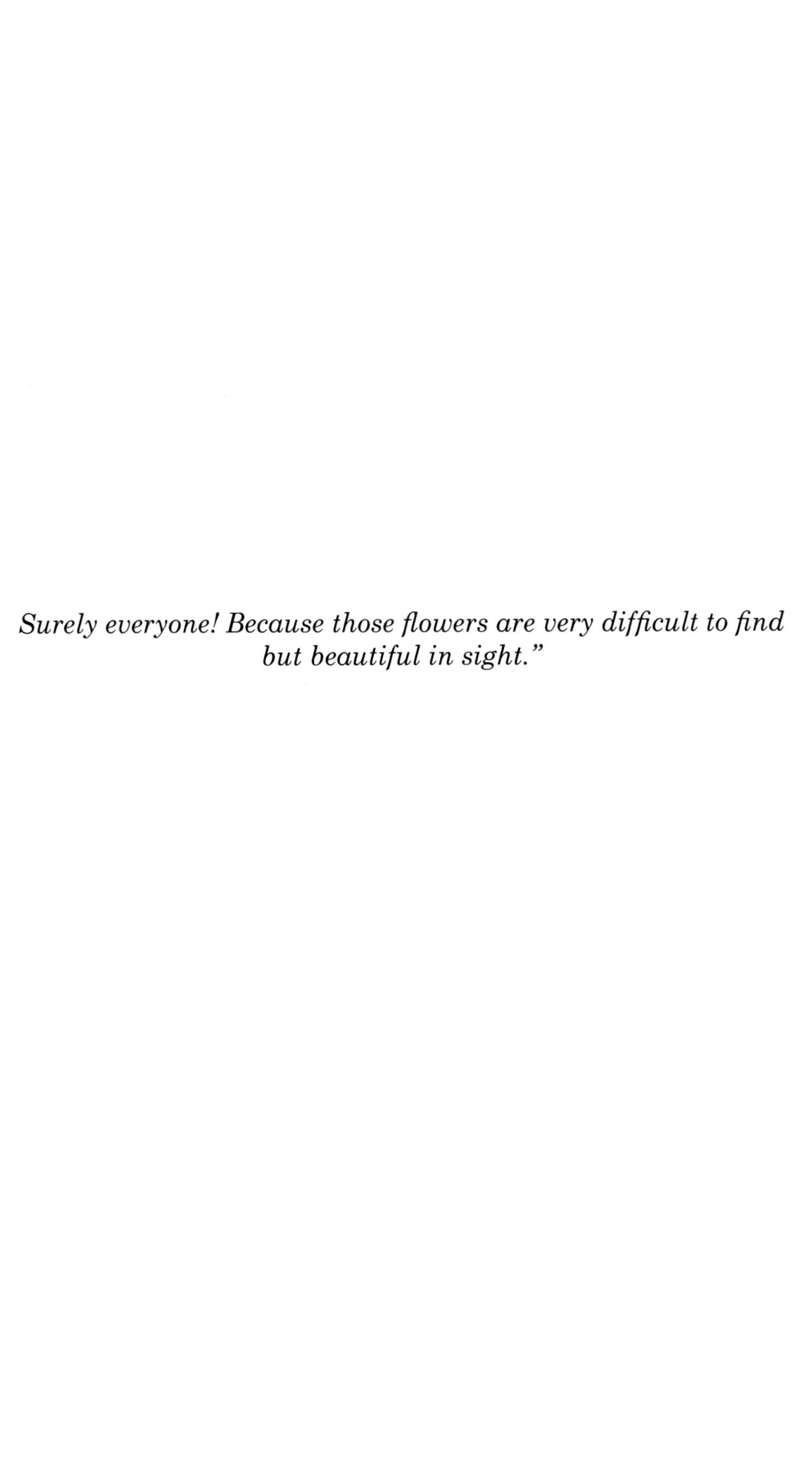

Surely everyone! Because those flowers are very difficult to find but beautiful in sight."

"There are also black eyes, black hair and skin with a radiant and beautiful tone like the night."

"Can you see now that we are all important, valuable, and deserve love and respect?

Do you realize that what really makes us valuable beings is not the appearance or what we possess?"

"The value of each human being is in the treatment and love we give to others."

"The true value lies within us, not on the outside."

"If you have siblings, you can realize that they are not entirely the same and your parents love them in the same way."
"Being different is not a crime or a sin. Being different doesn't change our value."

"Nature shows us different events every day, and there is beauty in each of them.

"Life can change us at any time, it may be that we look perfect and think that we will never need the help, or support of someone, but life can give us very hard and difficult lessons."

"You may not miss anything today, but maybe tomorrow you will lack an eye, a foot, a hand, or maybe just a friend to talk to."

"Being born with some difference does not make us different, it makes us unique!"

"We are all valuable and important. We all deserve love and respect.

We all have the ability to do magic! Because we are magical beings full of wonderful gifts and infinite abilities."

"Let's show that we children, even when they are young, can do great things!"

"We are the heroes of the world and we have the weapons to change it."

"Let's shoot words of love and respect everywhere, let's flood the world with humility and compassion."

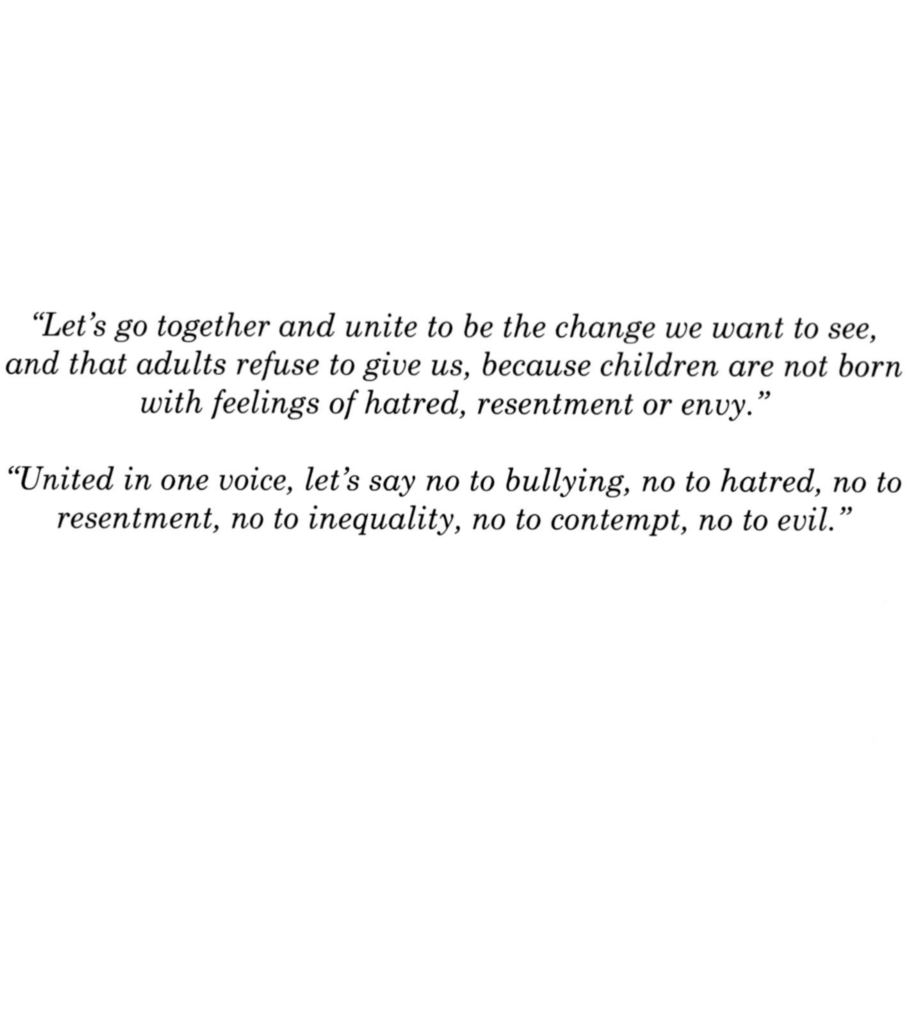

"Let's go together and unite to be the change we want to see, and that adults refuse to give us, because children are not born with feelings of hatred, resentment or envy."

"United in one voice, let's say no to bullying, no to hatred, no to resentment, no to inequality, no to contempt, no to evil."

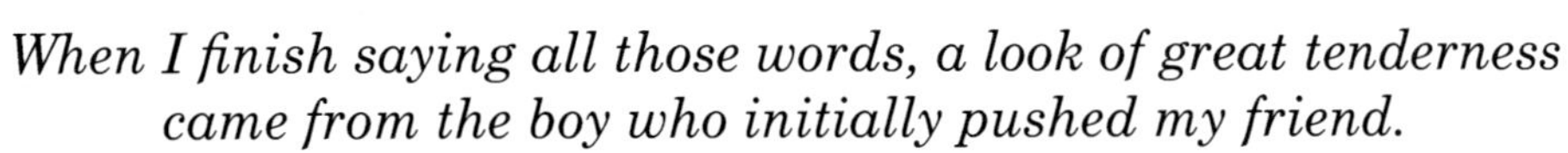

When I finish saying all those words, a look of great tenderness came from the boy who initially pushed my friend.

He took Santiago in his arms and they became one, they merged into a hug full of love and both shed tears that came from their souls. Tears that heal your pain and give you back love and hope.

We all ran and merged into a single hug, and promised never again to be the reason for a child to be afraid or shed tears.

This story that began with sadness and tears ended, and became love and smiles.

I, Laura, promise to give the best of myself to everyone in the world and I wish that we can all be that light of love and hope in the lives of others.

Let's learn to give love with the soul, and to look with our heart, because magic and true beauty is not visible with our eyes.

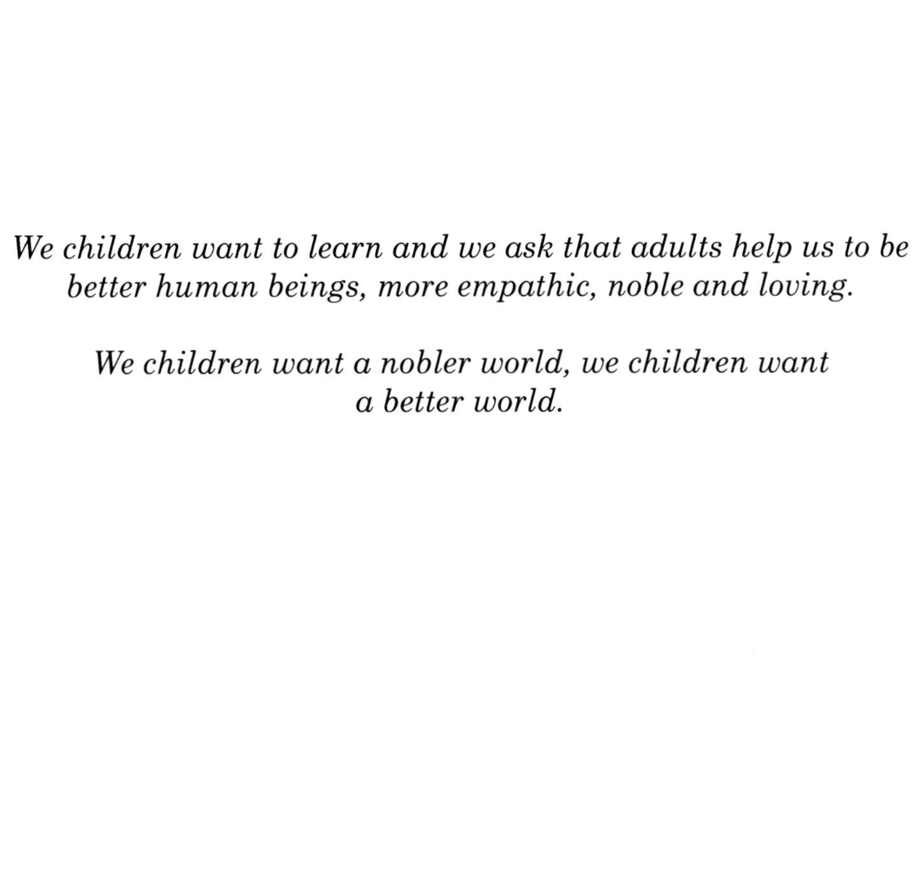

We children want to learn and we ask that adults help us to be better human beings, more empathic, noble and loving.

We children want a nobler world, we children want a better world.

No to Bullying, No to Racism

Made in the USA
Columbia, SC
28 May 2024

b7946d10-0a86-4ff9-9652-8eef501eda42R05